Seashore Babies

Kathy Darling
Photographs by Tara Darling

Walker and Company
New York

Grateful thanks to Alison Beall, naturalist at the Marshlands Conservancy in Rye, New York, whose mud walks always led us to horseshoe crabs.

To the Miami Seaquarium for allowing us to photograph the baby dolphin born to the costar of *Ace Ventura, Pet Detective*.

We should all give thanks that there are people like Harry and Darlene Kelton who have rescued and rehabilitated thousands of injured birds. We were privileged to photograph at their Pelican Harbor Seabird Station in Miami, Florida.

Thank you to Paul Dunnihoo, the manager of Monterey Bay Kayaks, a lover of all wild critters whose first-class transportation allowed us access to the sea otters of Monterey Bay, California. Thank you also to Paul Masaki and Dave Riley, the two skilled paddlers whose strong arms were matched only by their detailed knowledge of sea otter biology.

Appreciation to Vicki Sawyer of the Maritime Center in Norwalk, Connecticut, for locating sea stars and crabs.

To photographer Warren Rosenberg, who went sea-horsing around with us, and to the House of Fins in Greenwich, Connecticut, for providing us with beautiful minireef tanks for photography.

Text copyright © 1997 by Kathy Darling
Photographs copyright © 1997 by Tara Darling

First published in the United States of America in 1997 by Walker Publishing Company, Inc.
Published simultaneously in Canada by Thomas Allen & Son Canada, Limited, Markham, Ontario
Library of Congress Cataloging-in-Publication Data
Darling, Kathy.
Seashore Babies/Kathy Darling; photographs by Tara Darling.
p.   cm.
Summary: Photographs and text describe some of the young animals that are found at the seashore, including the sea lion, green turtle, and pelican.
ISBN 0-8027-8476-3 (hardcover). —ISBN 0-8027-8477-1 (reinforced)
1. Seashore animals—Juvenile literature. 2. Animals—Infancy—Juvenile literature. [1. Seashore animals.
2. Animals—Infancy.] I. Darling, Tara, ill. II. Title.
QL 122.2.D37   1997
591.3'9'09146—dc20   96-26951
CIP
AC
Illustration on page 3 and icons throughout the book by Dennis O'Brien.
Artwork on page 32 by Linda Howard and Elizabeth Sieferd.
Book design by Marva J. Martin.
Printed in Hong Kong
2 4 6 8 10 9 7 5 3 1

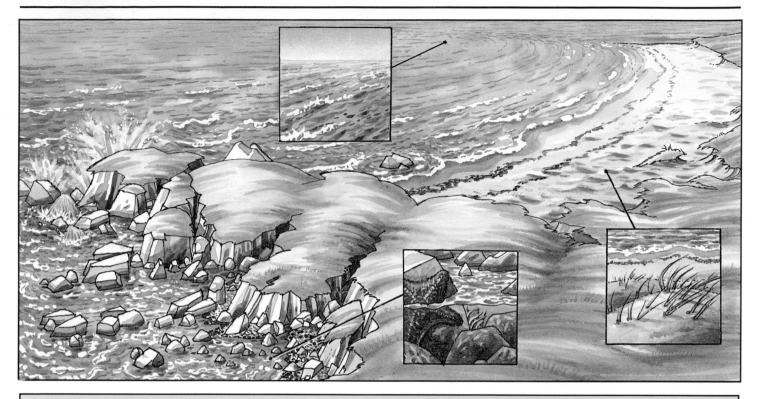

These symbols appear throughout the book and represent the zone along the seashore that each animal inhabits. For more information about these zones, turn to "About the Seashore" on the last page of the book.

COAST

TIDAL ZONE

SEA

Our home planet is called Earth. It probably should have been called Ocean. More than three quarters of the surface of our world is covered by life-giving water.

The ocean was home to the first living things. And it is still a good place for plants and animals to be born. Most sea life does not live in the cold, dark depths. It crowds against the land. Even animals that live most of their lives far from dry land come to the shore to have their babies.

Come and see what new life the tide has washed up on the beach. There are some adorable babies sleeping in the sand. And more swimming just offshore. Welcome to the wet zone.

Gull

Hit the target and win a fish! When gull chicks are hungry, they have a special way of asking for food. They peck the red spot on a parent's beak. This is a food target. When the baby hits it, mother or father gull will give it some fish to eat.

Parents work hard but they can't bring enough food to fill a five-week-old chick like the one on this page. The hungry baby must find some of its own fish. And that means learning to fly! Student pilots have crazy crashes and slam dunks into the sea at first. But gull parents stand by with emergency fish dinners till the chicks get the hang of flying.

Gull
(Herring Gull)

★ Baby name: Chick
★ Birthplace: Beach dunes or rocky ledges in a nest made of sticks, seaweed, and other vegetation
★ Birth size: 1 ounce
★ Adult size: 1 pound, 22 inches from head to tail
★ Littermates: 2 or 3
★ Favorite food: Fish, crabs, clams, and other marine tidbits. Gulls are two-legged sanitation squads, eating any dead things that wash up on the beach.
★ Parent care: Both parents sit on the eggs and help feed the chicks.
★ Enemies: Other gulls
★ Home: Atlantic and Pacific coasts of North America

Pelican

Go ahead and call a pelican "big mouth." It's not an insult. It's a pelican compliment. The big mouth, with stretchy skin attached to the lower half of the bill, is a giant scoop for catching fish.

A pelican chick, like the one on the facing page, needs more than a big bill to be a good fisherman. It is important for a fisherman to know what a fish looks like. Pelican babies don't, and they proudly catch leaves, seaweed, and sticks at first. But by watching mother and father pelican, they learn to spot fish from the sky, and dive into the water and scoop them up.

Pelican
(Brown Pelican)

ENDANGERED SPECIES

★ Baby name: Chick
★ Birthplace: Nest in a colony on beach or in low trees
★ Birth size: About as big as a baby chicken (2 ounces)
★ Adult size: 8 pounds, 3 1/2 feet long, including a 13-inch beak
★ Littermates: 2
★ Favorite food: Fish
★ Parent care: Both parents sit on the eggs and bring fish to the chicks for 18 weeks.
★ Enemies: Humans
★ Home: Atlantic and Pacific coasts of North America and Pacific coast of South America

Penguin

Home alone! Every day fairy penguin chicks are left alone in their seaside homes. The babies wait all morning and afternoon for their parents to come home with a tasty fish dinner. They are very hungry and complain loudly when the parade of parent penguins comes waddling ashore each evening.

Did you notice that adult fairy penguins are blue? That's not because they're cold. There is no ice or snow where the tiny birds live. For them, dull blue is a good camouflage color. Chicks, born with fluffy gray feathers, will get the waterproof blue ones in about two months. Then they will not have to stay home alone anymore.

Penguin
(Fairy Penguin)

★ Baby name: Chick
★ Birthplace: Rocky crevice or burrow dug underneath beach grass
★ Birth size: 1 1/3 ounce
★ Adult size: 2 to 4 pounds, 15 inches high
★ Littermates: 1 or 2
★ Favorite food: Fish
★ Parent care: Both parents bring food to the chicks for eight weeks.
★ Enemies: On land: wild cats, foxes, snakes; in the water: sharks, seals, sea lions
★ Home: Southern Australia and New Zealand

Sea Lion

Mother sea lions are swimming coaches. Their job isn't easy, because their pups are afraid of the water. The first lessons are in shallow tide pools so the baby doesn't get scared. After the pup has learned to dogpaddle, Coach Mom lures it to deeper water by playing games. "Shake the Seaweed" is everybody's favorite.

When they are not teaching swimming, sea lion mothers go fishing, often for several days. The pups stay together in nursery play groups, goofing off on the beach or practicing swimming along the shore.

"Are you my mother?" the hungry pups ask each returning cow, for only their own mom will give them milk.

This picture of a big male (above) reveals how these seals got the name sea *lion*.

Sea Lion
(Australian Sea Lion)

★ Baby name: Pup or calf
★ Birthplace: Rocky or sandy beach
★ Birth size: 12 pounds, 2 1/2 feet long
★ Adult size: Males: 750 to 850 pounds, 7 feet long; females: 200 pounds, 6 feet long
★ Littermates: Sometimes 1
★ Favorite food: Babies drink milk for almost a year, adding fish at about nine months.
★ Parent care: Mother nurses baby and teaches it how to swim and hunt.
★ Enemies: Humans, great white sharks
★ Home: Sandy and rocky beaches of Southern Australia

Seal

This is the start of something big. Baby elephant seals like the three-month-old pup on the facing page will grow and grow *and grow*, till they are the size of a car. Elephant seals are on the Top Ten list of animal heavyweights.

These two-and-a-half-ton sea mammals can dive deeper than any other air-breathing animal. Even deeper than whales.

A pup like this one, dusting his back with sand to repel insects, can dive 1,800 feet. But that is just kid stuff compared to his father's 5,000-foot plunges.

By the way, don't get into a breath-holding contest. Elephant seal pups have been known to go two hours between breaths!

Seal
(Northern Elephant Seal)

ENDANGERED SPECIES

★ Baby name: Pup
★ Birthplace: Sandy or rocky beach
★ Birth size: 70 pounds (weaners weigh over 300 pounds), 3 to 4 feet long
★ Adult size: Males: 5,000 pounds, 15 feet; females: 1,500 pounds, 9 feet
★ Littermates: None
★ Favorite food: Babies drink milk for a month and then eat fish.
★ Parent care: Mother nurses baby for four weeks and then abandons it.
★ Enemies: Sharks, killer whales, humans
★ Home: Beaches on the coast and offshore islands of California and Baja Mexico

COAST

Tern

T he sooty tern is one of the most common birds in the world. There are about 10 billion of these black-and-white sea birds. You might not ever see one of them, though. They only hang around land long enough to lay eggs and raise their babies.

Sooty terns live in the air. Really. Once this chick (facing page) gets off the ground, it will fly without stopping for ten years. Not once will it set down, either on land or water, until it is ready to have a family. It will sleep with the wind and eat on the wing, plucking fish from the surface of the ocean.

Tern
(Sooty Tern)

★ Baby name: Chick
★ Birthplace: Nest of twigs and leaves on beach sand or in seaside trees
★ Birth size: 1 ounce
★ Adult size: 7 ounces, 16 inches long
★ Littermates: None
★ Favorite food: Fish, especially flying fish
★ Parent care: Both parents incubate the egg and help feed the chick.
★ Enemies: Gulls and other meat-eating sea birds
★ Home: Air above the sea—except for breeding, which is done in huge colonies on ocean shores

Turtle

A hundred brothers? Or a hundred sisters? Whether a baby sea turtle has brothers or sisters depends on the temperature of the eggs. Normally there will be equal numbers of male and female turtles. But if the mother (right) has placed her nest in a sunny spot, all the hatchlings will be brothers. A shady nest will be a girls-only one.

A little turtle needs lots of brothers or sisters. It can't dig out of the deep nest alone. Only by working together can the babies make it to the surface. Then it's every turtle for itself as the hatchlings make a danger-filled dash to the sea, which will be their home for the rest of their lives.

Turtle
(Green Sea Turtle)

ENDANGERED SPECIES

★ Baby name: Hatchling
★ Birthplace: Sandy beach
★ Birth size: 1 ounce, 2 inches long
★ Adult size: 400 pounds; shell measures 3 to 4 feet from front to back
★ Littermates: 50 to 150
★ Favorite food: Babies eat jellyfish and other small sea creatures; adults are vegetarians, eating only algae and seaweed.
★ Parent care: None
★ Enemies: For eggs and babies, lizards, gulls, crabs, crocodiles, and fish are dangers; adult turtles' enemies are sharks and humans.
★ Home: Tropical seas around the world

Horseshoe Crab

A baby horseshoe crab grows so fast, it pops right out of its skin. It has to. A skin made of shell won't stretch. This hatchling (facing page), just over one year old, has exchanged its outgrown armor for a bigger size six times. The empty horseshoe crab shells you may find on the beach are probably not dead animals but outgrown skins. (Look for a slit in the front where the growing baby wiggled out.)

The tanklike animals look like crabs, but they are really relatives of spiders. Designed millions of years ago, horseshoe crabs look scary, but there is no reason to be frightened. They have no claws to pinch you and no teeth to bite you, and the spiky tail is just a tool to help them flip over.

Horseshoe Crab
(American Horseshoe Crab)

- ★ Baby name: Hatchling, trilobite larva
- ★ Birthplace: Sandy tide pool
- ★ Birth size: 1/8 inch across the shell
- ★ Adult size: Females weigh 3 pounds and are 2 feet long; males are about half the size of females.
- ★ Littermates: Thousands
- ★ Favorite food: Babies eat tiny bacteria and floating microscopic animals called plankton. Adults eat worms, crustaceans, mollusks.
- ★ Parent care: None
- ★ Enemies: For eggs, birds; for young, worms, jellyfish, clams. Adult crabs are sometimes caught by humans (for medical research).
- ★ Home: Atlantic coast of North America

Sea Star

Walking isn't easy if you have five feet and each one is pointing in a different direction. Some sea stars have a favorite foot and always step off with it. Others begin with whatever foot is pointing in the direction they want to go. Once the choice is made, thousands of movable suction cups on the underside of each foot pull the sea star along.

New sea stars are created in two very different ways. Some begin as babies that hatch from eggs. Others are never really babies. They are created when a grown-up loses one of its feet. Two complete sea stars will result from the accident. The body makes a new foot. That's amazing. But even more amazing is what happens to the broken-off foot. It becomes a whole new star by growing four matching feet, a body, and a brain!

Sea Star
(Common Sea Star)

★ Baby name: Larva
★ Birthplace: Sea
★ Birth size: Tiny—about as big as a pencil point
★ Adult size: There are 2,000 species of sea stars that range from 1/2 inch to 3 feet across. The common sea star, which lives on the northeast coast of the United States, grows to about 8 inches.
★ Littermates: Millions
★ Favorite food: Larva eat tiny bacteria and plankton. Adults eat the meat of clams, worms, oysters, mussels, and sea urchins.
★ Parent care: Mothers protect eggs. Care ends when the larvae hatch.
★ Enemies: Mainly humans, who compete for the same food
★ Home: Tide pools and shallow waters—with some species being adapted to deep-sea bottoms around the world

SEA **TIDAL ZONE**

Crab

With long skinny legs and tiny claws, this baby looks more like a spider than a crab. Looks gave it its name. Its habits gave it its nickname—decorator crab. When they are young, these ten-legged designers make themselves into an art project. Each decorator sticks bits of seaweed and sponges on its back. The dressed-up crabs are sometimes pretty, but more important, the decorations help them hide from crab eaters.

Some species of spider crabs, like this one (facing page), have another decorating skill. They can change the color of their shells to match their surroundings.

Crab
(Spider Crab)

★ Baby name: Hatchling, larva
★ Birthplace: Tide pool or shallow water
★ Birth size: Tiny—as big as a pencil point
★ Adult size: This species is 8 inches from leg tip to leg tip. There are 200 species of spider crabs; the largest of them spans 12 feet.
★ Littermates: Hundreds
★ Favorite food: Rotting plants and animals
★ Parent care: None
★ Enemies: Birds, fish, octopus, squid
★ Home: Shallow waters of northeastern United States

Dolphin

A baby dolphin (facing page) gets to pick its own name. As soon as it is born, the infant whistles its name to its mother. She whistles hers back. Then grandma dolphin introduces herself to the newborn. Soon the whole family is calling out their whistle names.

A whistle name is like a signature. Every one is different. The members of a dolphin herd "talk" to each other with whistles and more than 40 other sounds. Their conversations are full of quacks, barks, blats, squawks, and squeals. Dolphins also make clicking noises, which help them locate fish. Babies don't go fishing until they get some teeth. This year-old calf has just gotten the first of its 180 fish grabbers.

Dolphin
(Bottlenose Dolphin)

ENDANGERED SPECIES

★ Baby name: Calf
★ Birthplace: Ocean
★ Birth size: 70 pounds, 3 1/2 feet
★ Adult size: 450 pounds, 7 feet
★ Littermates: None
★ Favorite food: Milk for 18 months, then fish, squid, eels, worms, and even hermit crabs
★ Parent care: Mother protects baby for up to six years.
★ Enemies: Humans, sharks, killer whales
★ Home: Warm parts of the oceans of the world. Bottlenose dolphins usually stay close to shore.

SEA

Manatee

Newborn manatees drink only milk. But soon the calves are nibbling on the sea grasses their mothers eat. Manatee cows don't nibble, they gobble. The largest vegetarians in the sea, each of these mammals chomps its way through 200 pounds of sea grass and weeds every day.

If any of that grass gets stuck between their teeth, it drives the manatees crazy. So they clean their teeth after every meal. Manatees have invented some very clever ways to brush underwater. Some try to sweep the bits out with a flipper. Some use fish as living toothpicks. And gargling with rocks is very popular. If all else fails, a manatee will floss with a boat's anchor line. This works, but it's dangerous to swim near boats. The slow-moving manatees are often killed or injured by the motors.

Manatee
(West Indian Manatee)

ENDANGERED SPECIES

★ Baby name: Calf
★ Birthplace: Shallow waters
★ Birth size: 60 pounds, 3 feet long
★ Adult size: 1,200 pounds, 10 feet long
★ Littermates: None
★ Favorite food: Babies drink milk for several years; adults eat sea grasses and freshwater plants.
★ Parent care: Mother takes care of baby for two years. Father does not help.
★ Enemies: Humans, sharks
★ Home: Tropical waters of Florida and the Caribbean

Otter

Baby sea otters have to get tied up at bedtime. Before a pup goes to sleep in its ocean cradle, Mother wraps it tightly in ropes made of giant seaweed. This is not a punishment. It's safety at sea. Unless otters are tied to the strongly anchored seaweed, they might drift far from shore during the night. A baby might even get separated from its mother.

The five-month-old pup above is wrapped in the weeds for a little nap. The tiny baby on the facing page being groomed by its mother is only one week old. It's too little to sleep alone. Mother otter will hold it in her arms.

Otter
(Sea Otter)

ENDANGERED SPECIES

★ Baby name: Pup
★ Birthplace: Ocean
★ Birth size: 4 to 5 pounds, 15 inches long
★ Adult size: Up to 120 pounds, 3 to 4 feet long, plus a 15-inch tail
★ Littermates: None
★ Favorite food: Babies drink milk for almost a year; adults eat urchins, crabs, mussels, and abalone.
★ Parent care: Mother feeds, grooms, and protects baby. Father does not help.
★ Enemies: Humans, sharks, killer whales
★ Home: Northern Pacific—Alaska, Russia, and a small population in northern California

SEA

Sea Horse

Baby sea horses, like the one on the facing page, look just like their daddy when he gives birth to them. The small fry hatch from eggs that the father carries in a pouch on his belly. When they pop out, the newborn sea horses are really hungry. For a snack, these month-old babies might suck three or four thousand tiny shrimp into their long snout.

Sea horses aren't very good swimmers. Tiny fins on their neck and back barely move them along. But they can do something no other fish can: They can hold on with their tails. When they have a good hitching post, sea horses can hang motionless and ambush their dinner.

Sea Horse
(Northern Giant Sea Horse)

★ Baby name: Hatchling or fry
★ Birthplace: Underwater grass fields or shallow coral reefs
★ Birth size: 1/2 inch long: small fry grow fast, doubling their size in a week
★ Adult size: 8 inches long
★ Littermates: Up to 150
★ Favorite food: Babies eat tiny shrimp, worms, and fish eggs; adults eat bigger shrimp and worms.
★ Parent care: Father keeps eggs in pouch on his belly. He does not protect the babies after they hatch.
★ Enemies: Humans who destroy habitat and collect them for aquariums
★ Home: Seashores of the western Atlantic

About the Seashore

Earth is a water world. Great seas averaging two and a half miles in depth cover most of the planet's surface. It is in this watery cradle where most life forms began and still live. They are not spread evenly throughout the oceans. Ninety percent of marine plants and animals are found in the meeting places between land and water.

In *shallow coastal seas* there is sunlight and plenty of food for plants. Underwater forests of giant seaweed grow as much as a foot a day. Floating gardens bloom with microscopic organisms called plankton. The shore-hugging waters with their rich feeding grounds attract small plant-eating fish and the bigger fish and animals that eat them.

The *tidal zone* is a world of specially adapted creatures not really a part of the ocean, yet not belonging to the land either. Every shore in the world has a tidal zone created by the gravitational pull that the moon and the sun exert on the Earth. It can be a rocky pool a few inches deep or a mud flat hundreds of feet wide. But always it is bathed twice each day as the sea rhythmically advances and retreats.

Above the tide line is the *coast*. Coasts vary widely, and so does the life that lives on them. Some shores are pounded by twenty-foot waves that hurl themselves against the land, climbing cliffs and gradually grinding rocks into sand. A few hardy creatures thrive there. A bigger group of life forms live along coasts with gentler waves and muddy or sandy shores.

The babies in each of these zones face different challenges.
But they all call the seashore home.